W9-CJG-923

A BEACON • BIOGRAPHY

John Boyega

Tamra B. Orr

PURPLE TOAD
PUBLISHING

Copyright © 2017 by Purple Toad Publishing, Inc. All rights reserved. No part of this book may be reproduced without written permission from the publisher. Printed and bound in the United States of America.

Printing   1   2   3   4   5   6   7   8   9

A Beacon Biography

Angelina Jolie
Big Time Rush
Cam Newton
Carly Rae Jepsen
Daisy Ridley
Drake
Ed Sheeran
Ellen DeGeneres
Elon Musk
Harry Styles of One Direction
Jennifer Lawrence
John Boyega
Kevin Durant
Lorde
Malala
Maria von Trapp
Markus "Notch" Persson, Creator of Minecraft
Mo'ne Davis
Muhammad Ali
Neil deGrasse Tyson
Peyton Manning
Robert Griffin III (RG3)

Publisher's Cataloging-in-Publication Data
Orr, Tamra.
    John Boyega / written by Tamra B. Orr.
        p. cm.
Includes bibliographic references, glossary, and index.
ISBN 9781624692864
1. Boyega, John, 1992- — Juvenile literature. 2. Motion picture actors and actresses — United States--Biography — Juvenile literature. I. Series: Beacon biography.
 PN2287 2017
 791.43

Library of Congress Control Number: 2016936451

eBook ISBN: 9781624692871

ABOUT THE AUTHOR: Tamra B. Orr is a full-time author living in the Pacific Northwest. She has written more than 450 educational books for readers of all ages. She is a graduate of Ball State University and commonly gives presentations to schools and conferences. She remembers going to the first *Star Wars* movie back in 1977 and still enjoys the stories decades later. As a fan, she always preferred Han Solo to Luke Skywalker, but admits Finn is an excellent addition to the cast.

PUBLISHER'S NOTE: This story has not been authorized or endorsed by John Boyega.

CONTENTS

John Boyega

Damilola Taylor's parents set up a trust in their son's name, as well as a center in Peckham that provides access to sports and community activities to youth.

A Life Lost Too Soon

It was over in an instant. One moment John Boyega, his sister Grace, and ten-year-old Damilola Taylor were talking, and the next Damilola was in big trouble.

John, Grace, and Damilola were more than just classmates. They were friends. The three often walked home from school and the library together. Damilola had moved to London from Nigeria only a few months before, and the Boyegas wanted to make sure he knew his way around. "Damilola and John and Grace were so close," Richard Taylor, Damilola's father, told *The Mirror*. "They were looking after him when he arrived in the U.K."[1] As usual, on this afternoon, the Boyegas offered to walk their new friend home. Today he said no thanks, he would go alone. It was the biggest—and last—mistake he would ever make.

"They left him by the junction then he went around the corner," explained Taylor, "and the gang was waiting for him."[2] Minutes later, young Taylor was attacked. Twelve- and thirteen-year-old brothers Danny and Ricky Preddie slashed him with a piece of broken glass. Although an ambulance came for Damilola, he died on the way to the hospital.

Grace was terribly saddened by the news. "After Damilola first arrived at the school, I was the one who showed him around and we paired up," she

Damilola Taylor

told *The Sun*. "He was so bubbly and enthusiastic, always smiling. When the teacher told us Damilola had died, I just couldn't stop crying."[3]

The Boyegas deeply missed their friend, but John was not surprised when he heard the news. In the North Peckham area where he grew up, gang violence was common. "The reality is there was a lot of trouble where I grew up," he told *The Irish Daily Star*. "The estate [development] I grew up in, in Peckham, was one of the worst in London."[4] In the Boyega's neighborhood, gangs, guns, knives, and death were daily threats.

Fortunately, John and his two older sisters, Grace and Blessing, were not tempted to be part of that dangerous lifestyle. "I was never even tempted by crime…," John told *The Star*. "I never had any interest in gangs or criminal activities."[5]

It took six years for the Preddie brothers to be arrested and tried in court. During those years, Richard Taylor never forgot the kindness the Boyega family showed his son. John did not forget the Taylor family, either. He invited the entire Taylor family to the London premiere of *Star Wars: The Force Awakens*. Boyega also made sure that some of the money raised by the Star Wars: Force for Change foundation went to the Damilola

Blessing Boyega has been a model for many years.

Taylor Trust. This organization is dedicated to helping and supporting young people in South London. In a video on the charity's web site, Boyega states, "I will be supporting the Damilola Taylor Trust. It's a great charity that gives opportunities to young people and it's something that inspired me throughout my whole life, so I'm very proud. . . . May the force be with you."[6]

At the premiere, Richard Taylor beamed with pride at how far John had come since those long-ago days of elementary school. "There's good coming out of this place," said Taylor, referring to the Peckham area. "John's promoting Peckham, not denying his roots. Damilola would have been doing the same thing."[7]

Richard Taylor knows that his son would have achieved great things, if he had only had the chance.

The neighborhood where John Boyega grew up was dangerous, but the future Stormtrooper found his answer to survival.

Staying Out of Trouble

Growing up in a rough neighborhood is never easy, but John Boyega found a way to push trouble aside and focus on something that had become very important to him: acting.

When Boyega was born on March 17, 1992, he joined parents Samson and Abigail, as well as two older sisters, Grace and Blessing. Samson was a minister, and Abigail worked with children with learning disabilities.

When his elementary school decided to put on a school play, John was chosen for the part of the leopard. "I went on all fours, and I was playing this leopard," Boyega recalled in an article with *Interview* magazine, "and I gave him character breakdown, and I was doing the work and doing the research and creating a character. That is the greatest feeling ever," he added. "When you're young and you're like, 'Oh, this is quite cool, and I really, really, want to do this.'"[1]

From the moment he played a leopard, Boyega's decision was made. He was going to be an actor. When he was only nine years old, Teresa Early, the director of Theatre Peckham, saw him in a play and knew she was seeing someone with talent. "I saw him and thought, 'Oh, that boy has something,' "

Even when he was young, Boyega (left) shone on the stage.

she recalled to *The Telegraph*.[2] She quickly invited young Boyega to be a part of a special program for students ages nine through fourteen at the theater. He was thrilled.

Boyega did not tell his friends or classmates about the hours he spent after school and on weekends taking drama classes and going to rehearsals. One of his friends stated, "Everyone else does football (soccer) when they're young. John didn't play football, he was more interested in acting, so he didn't want to make a big fuss about it."[3]

One person who was not pleased about Boyega's passion for acting was his father. As a minister, Samson had hoped his son would follow in his footsteps and become a minister also. He grew tired of his son's involvement with the drama school, but eventually he changed his mind. "I had a chat with John's father when he was about 12 or 13," said Early, the theater program director. "As long as John stayed out of trouble, they [his parents]

were quite happy. And as John made his way, his father began to think there was some wisdom in it."[4]

Many of Boyega's friends thought he made the right decision in focusing on acting. A neighbor stated, "You would never see John on the street or hanging around gangs." A friend added, "A lot of boys in his year are now in prison or dead. Everyone was going down one route towards the end of school—taking drugs, selling drugs, gangs, that sort of thing—but John went down another. I am so thankful he got out of it."[5]

It took a while for father Samson to agree to his son's acting, but he eventually did.

Boyega loved performing. "While so many kids where I lived were getting involved in gang activity, I was more interested in Shakespeare," he told *The Daily Star*. "There weren't many kids from where I lived that dreamed to play Othello, but since acting in primary school, I caught the bug and knew it was what I wanted."[6]

After his years with the Peckham Theatre, Boyega attended South Thames College, majoring in performing arts. He then attended the Identity School of Acting, the United Kingdom's leading part-time drama school, for three years. He appeared in several plays, including the lead in *Othello*.

Although he enrolled in Greenwich University, Boyega found he did not have enough time for classes. Why? His acting career was already taking off—and was about to go all the way to the stars.

Abigail Boyega was quite proud of her son as well.

Attack the Block *was the story of some very unlikely heroes.*

Finding Jobs and Fighting Aliens

Boyega's years of playing everything from fierce leopards to Shakespearian characters paid off in 2011. Boyega was hired by Film 4 Productions to make an independent science fiction movie called *Attack the Block*. He would play Moses, the teenage leader of five street kids from South London. A troublemaker at first, Moses becomes the hero in a battle against fast, furry, neon blue–toothed aliens.

Attack the Block was Boyega's first starring role and he had great fun with it. He told *Interview* magazine that being in the movie made him feel like a little kid again. "[It] was incredibly fun," he said. "I just always compare it to being a kid and running around, and imagining things that aren't there. It's the same thing, just in a professional, controlled environment."[1]

Attack the Block was a huge hit with the critics. However, it was not a big hit with audiences during it's theatrical release. It played in only a few theaters throughout the United Kingdom, and it was even harder to find in the United States. Although the movie was very well done, and the cast, including Boyega, was excellent, there was almost no advertising for it. No commercials were run on television. Like many favorites through the years, it has since become a cult favorite around the world—thanks to home video—and is much loved by science fiction fans today.

Boyega's role in the science fiction cult hit earned him awards—and Hollywood attention.

In an actor profile on TribecaFilm.com, the reviewer describes Boyega's Moses as a "fearless, natural-born leader" and already looking like an action star.[2] In one of the most exciting scenes of the movie, caught in slow motion, Moses runs down a hallway, music blaring, a sword raised in his hand. For his role in *Attack the Block*, Boyega was nominated for many awards. He won the London Film Critics' Circle Award for Young British Performer of the Year.

Soon after his debut in *Attack the Block*, Boyega was asked to star in a HBO boxing drama called *Da Brick*. Produced by Spike Lee, the story would center on a young man named Donnie, played by Boyega. It was loosely based on the story of boxer Mike Tyson. In the end, HBO turned down the series.

It was disappointing for Boyega, but it certainly did not slow him down. Between 2011 and 2014, he starred in the movies *Junkhearts* as a drug dealer, *Half of a Yellow Sun* as a houseboy named Ugwu during the 1960s civil war in Nigeria, and *Imperial Dreams* as a reformed gangster trying to put his life back together after getting out of prison.

Along with movie roles, Boyega was also cast as Danny Curtis in the BBC's TV series *Becoming Human*, and as First Lieutenant Chris Tanner in several episodes of *24: Live Another Day*. In addition, he was in an episode of *Law and Order: UK*, as well as in the TV movie *My Murder*.

Many people watched Boyega save the day in *Attack the Block*. One of those people was the famous movie director and producer J.J. Abrams. When he saw Boyega rescuing his city from lethal aliens, he was impressed. "I met J.J. a few years ago," Boyega recalled to *The Mary Sue*. "J.J. just goes to me, 'You know what, John? I loved you in *Attack the Block*. We're going to get you something.'"[3] Boyega was stunned—and thrilled.

Four years later, that "something" turned out to be one of the biggest roles in movie history. As Boyega said, "[H]e got me in something. It just happened to be *Star Wars*. So I like that guy."[4]

J.J. Abrams knew Boyega was a talented actor and had just the right role for him.

Like Han Solo in the original films, Boyega's Finn is a reluctant hero.

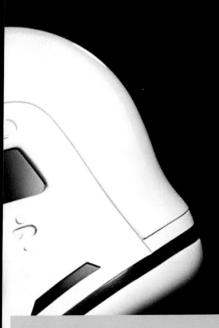

Becoming a Stormtrooper

From the time Boyega was a child, he was a *Star Wars* fan—although he actually preferred the Dark Side. In an interview with *GQ* magazine, he admitted he played with many *Star Wars* toys, but his favorite was Darth Vader. "He was the only toy from my collection that looked slightly evil," he stated. "It's not interesting if you don't have a bad guy."[1] In addition, he read all of the comic books and watched all of the movies. Little could he have known that when he was 23 years old, he would be one of the lead stars in the seventh movie of the series, *Star Wars: The Force Awakens*.

Boyega was not just handed the role of Finn, the stormtrooper who changes sides and becomes a hero in the film. He worked hard for it. "When I found out I had the part," he told *Vogue*, "the overwhelming feeling was of relief. I'd been auditioning for seven months so it was just unbelievable to think, yes, finally, I know I'm sure I'm going to be in this film."[2] He also told *GQ* that auditioning was "like *The X Factor* but without the TV show around it. It was intense."[3] (*The X Factor* is a televised competition that aims to find new musical talent.)

When Boyega first read the script for the new film, he admitted that he cried. "I'm not really a big crier," he told *GQ*. "I'm more like a frog-in-the-throat kind of guy, who'll try to hold it in and make sure I don't let it all out."[4] Fearing he would end up not getting the role, Boyega didn't even tell his parents he

Boyega recognized that he had just gotten the role of a lifetime as the stormtrooper Finn.

was trying out for it. "Telling them about a possibility of a dream and if you don't get it, they will be so heartbroken," he explained to *Access Hollywood Life.*[5]

The day Boyega found out he had won the role of Finn was one the young actor will always remember. "I cried. I was sobbing," he recalled. "This is after seven months of auditioning, so it's like you don't know whether your life is going to change or you go back to how your life used to be."[6]

As excited as he was to get the role, his parents were not so sure, as they knew little about the entire *Star Wars* saga. They had never seen a *Star Wars* movie. "My dad had no clue," Boyega stated on *Access Hollywood*. "But he was still excited. I mean, he was over the moon that his son had a job."[7] In his *GQ* interview, Boyega added that when he told them he had been hired, his parents were enthusiastic. "[T]hey said, 'Wow. This must be a big deal.' I said, 'Yes, Mom and Dad, this is huge!' They're very, very happy because I was happy."[8]

Being Finn was a thrill from beginning to end for Boyega. "Finn is dope. His story is so epic," he told *GQ*. "It's a story that's never been seen before, but it also mirrors the stories of Luke Skywalker and Han Solo. And he's quirky and charismatic and funny. For me, he was the best character in the script."

The movie was also exhausting. Boyega admitted the light sabers are challenging to use. "They're heavy, those things, and there's a lot of running involved. I was trained on a high-incline treadmill, so when it came to it I could spring around the desert in a leather jacket. They should do a Star Wars weight loss program," he added with a grin.[9]

In addition to getting fit enough to handle its physical demands, Boyega also had to lose his British accent for the role. "It's not the first film that I've

With all the lines, the action, and the fencing training (for duels using a light sabre), being Finn was demanding.

had an American accent in," he told *Vogue*, "so I had some practice, but it's definitely something I worked hard on and really wanted it to feel natural."[10] He also told *Esquire*, "I felt like it fitted the character well."[11]

Filming *Star Wars: The Force Awakens* allowed Boyega to work with some of the most famous actors in movie history. He and Daisy Ridley, the actor who plays Rey in the movie, became close friends. Boyega also grew close to actor Harrison Ford, who plays Han Solo in the *Star Wars* movies. Boyega said working with Ford was a dream come true. "Harrison is great to work with," he told *Vogue*. "It's hard not to admire him, not just as an actor but as a man. He's built an incredible career and being on set with him and learning from him is brilliant. Our characters had quite a lot of scenes together so it worked well that we had a good rapport."[12]

The new *Star Wars* movie has been a huge hit, breaking movie release records and bringing in over $2 billion worldwide. Boyega has gotten

Daisy and John both had to learn to not use their natural British accents in their movie roles.

No more clones: James Bond actor Daniel Craig played a stormtrooper in The Force Awakens in a scene with a captured Rey (Daisy Ridley).

tremendous reviews for his portrayal of Finn. He takes it in stride when the occasional fan of the Star Wars prequels tweets that because they were cloned in those films, stormtroopers are all supposed to be white.

In the original Star Wars trilogy, the stormtroopers were from many backgrounds. Years later, the creator of Star wars, George Lucas, made a new trilogy. Called "prequels" because they take place before the original stories do, these films showed the beginnings of the stormtroopers as clones of one single soldier, duplicated many times to populate an army. (The cloned stormtrooper in the prequels was played by Temuera Morrison, a Maori actor.) In the newest installment, the stormtroopers are no longer clones, but soldiers with their own feelings, relationships, opinions, and backgrounds. Some of them are white—and many are not. At least one is a woman named Captain Phasma.

At first, Boyega's response to the criticism, according to *The New York Times*, was, "I'm grounded in who I am, and I am a confident black man. I wasn't raised to fear people with a difference of opinion…. I'm not going to lose sleep."[13]

J.J. Abrams added, "All I know is John Boyega does an extraordinary job in the movie. The people who are complaining about that probably have bigger problems than, 'there's a black stormtrooper.' "[14]

Temuera Morrison

Boyega answers fan questions about the future at the San Diego Comic Con in 2015.

As Finn—and Beyond

What can an actor possibly do to top having a lead role in one of movie history's largest movies? Star in its sequel, of course.

Boyega was hired to play Finn in the next installment of the *Star Wars* legacy. The eighth movie would be released on December 15, 2017. During filming, its name and plot were tightly held secrets, but Boyega gave his fans a few clues in his interviews. When asked about the story, he told *Vogue*, "[We're] just staring work on *Star Wars VIII*, the next film, so I'm back to keeping secrets again. It's great. Much darker, but we're very excited."[1] He also hinted that as physical as his role was in *The Force Awakens*, the next movie would demand more from him. "My part in the next film will be much more physical, so I might be in the gym a bit more," he teased in the *Vogue* interview.[2]

Between finishing the seventh *Star Wars* movie and filming for the eighth, Boyega kept busy. He provided the voice for the character of Blkmrkt, a computer hacker, in the animated *Major Lazer* series. He also provides the voice for the character of Dutch in the Nickelodeon animated series *Tinkershrimp & Dutch*. Dutch is a slow loris, a small tree-dwelling primate with large eyes and no tail. Dutch and Tinkershrimp, a langoustine, or small lobster, are best friends. In each episode, the two creatures time travel in a castle on wheels called the Royal Double Decker.

In 2016, Boyega appeared in the science-fiction movie *The Circle* as Ty, the founder of a futuristic company. His costars included Harry Potter's Emma Watson, *Guardians of the Galaxy*'s Karen Gillan, and seasoned actor Tom Hanks. He also signed to star in a BBC-Netflix animated version of the children's classic *Watership Down*.

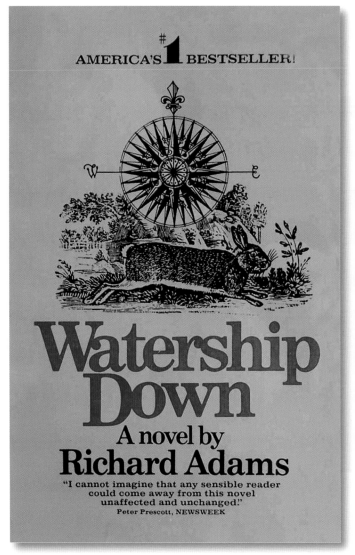

The cover of the classic novel **Watership Down.** *Often compared to epics like* **The Lord of the Rings,** *this novel is being produced as a mini-series for both the BBC and Netflix. It will feature the voices of not only Boyega (as the powerful Bigwig), but also of James McAvoy, Nicholas Hoult, Ben Kingsley, and Gemma Arterton.*

Along with acting, Boyega takes time out to surprise his fans. In March 2016, Boyega, dressed as his character Finn, went to the Royal London Hospital. He was there at the request of five-year-old *Star Wars* fan Daniel Bell. The little boy was coping with a brain tumor, and his biggest wish was to meet Boyega and help him hand out *Star Wars* related toys to all of the other kids at the hospital. The Rays of Sunshine Children's Charity reached out to the young actor, and he was happy to help.

Boyega told *The Daily Mail*, "When I heard about Daniel's wish to meet Finn, I jumped at the chance to make it come true. It was fantastic to be a part of his very special wish with Rays of Sunshine. It was great to meet the children at the Royal London Hospital and be a part of something so positive."[3]

Boyega thrills his young fans at the Royal London Hospital with a personal appearance and some fun gifts.

This was one special lightsaber duel for the young actor and his even younger fan.

In addition to handing out toys, Boyega and Daniel had a light-saber duel. Later Boyega posted on Instagram about his experience. "Really thankful for the opportunity this child granted me and I'm just humbled! I hope I played a little part in making you smile, young stormtrooper."[4]

Boyega has been in demand since Star Wars. Besides starring in the upcoming Pacific Rim II, Oscar-winning director Kathryn Bigelow (The Hurt Locker) has picked him for her new film. The drama will deal with the Detroit race riots of 1967.

In February 2016, Boyega won the Rising Star Award from BAFTA (British Academy of Film and Television Arts). He stood onstage, a huge smile lighting his face. According to *The Daily Mail*, he said, "Guys, I haven't been doing this for a long time, it's a fluke! I'm gonna share this award with all the young dreamers who are determined, who are hardworking, who are quite frankly amazing. This is also for you."[5] It was a humble moment for a star who is clearly going to keep rising.

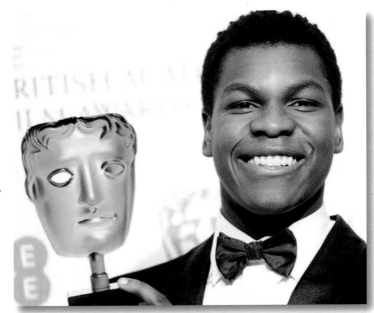

The only thing bigger than Boyega's smile was his pride at winning the BAFTA award.

1992   John Boyega is born on March 17 in Peckham, London, England. He has two older sisters, Grace and Blessing.

2000   John and Grace's ten-year-old friend Damilola Taylor is killed by two older boys.

2001   John joins Theatre Peckham.

2008   He studies performing arts at South Thames College, and then at the Identity School of Acting in Hackney.

2010   He lands a role in the vampire drama *Being Human*.

2011   He stars in his first film, *Attack the Block*. Boyega works with Spike Lee on the boxing series *Da Brick*, but the series does not air. Many other movie and television roles come his way.

2015   J.J. Abrams asks Boyega to try out for the role of Finn in *Star Wars: The Force Awakens*. After many months of auditioning, Boyega lands the role. He also does voice work in several animated series.

2016   Boyega plays Finn again in *Star Wars VIII*. He also works on *The Circle* and *Watership Down*.

FILMOGRAPHY

2018	*Pacific Rim II: Maelstrom*	**2015**	*Major Lazer* (animated series)
2017	*Star Wars VIII*		
	The Circle	**2014**	*24: Live Another Day* (TV miniseries)
	Watership Down (TV mini- series)	**2013**	*Half of a Yellow Sun*
2016	*Star Wars: The Force Awakens*	**2011**	*Attack the Block*
		2010	*Being Human* (TV series)
	Tinkershimp & Dutch (animated series)		

Chapter 1

1. Selby, Alan. "Star Wars Hero John Boyega Was Close Pals with Tragic Schoolboy Damilola Taylor." *The Mirror.* December 22, 2015. http://www.mirror.co.uk/tv/tv-news/star-wars-hero-john-boyega-7059437
2. Ibid.
3. Rollings, Grant. "Star Wars Actor's Secret: John Boyega Knew Tragic Damilola Taylor." *The Sun.* December 12, 2015. http://www.thesun.co.uk/sol/homepage/features/6542690/Star-Wars-John-Boyegas-family-was-close-to-Damilola-Taylor.html
4. Gleave, Ed. "Star Wars Actor John Boyega: 'I Grew Up with Deadly Gangs." *Irish Daily Star.* Undated. http://thestar.ie/star-wars-actor-john-boyega-i-grew-up-with-deadly-gangs/
5. Ibid.
6. Champion, Matthew. "Here's What We Know about John Boyega and Damilola Taylor." *BuzzFeed.* December 23, 2015. http://tinyurl.com/zjycygq
7. Selby.

Chapter 2

1. "The Attack of John Boyega." *Interview.* July 29, 2011. http://www.interviewmagazine.com/film/john-boyega-attack-the-block#_
2. Turner, Camilla. "Star Wars: Five Things You Didn't Know about John Boyega." *The Telegraph.* April 25, 2015. http://www.telegraph.co.uk/news/celebritynews/11562734/Star-Wars-Five-things-you-didnt-know-about-John-Boyega.html
3. Ibid.
4. Ibid.
5. Ibid.
6. Gleave, Ed. "Star Wars Actor John Boyega: 'I Grew Up with Deadly Gangs." *Irish Daily Star.* Undated. http://thestar.ie/star-wars-actor-john-boyega-i-grew-up-with-deadly-gangs/

Chapter 3

1. "The Attack of John Boyega." *Interview.* July 29, 2011. http://www.interviewmagazine.com/film/john-boyega-attack-the-block#_
2. Barone, Matt. "A Star Was Born: Before *Star Wars: The Force Awakens,* There Was *Attack the Block*." TribecaFilm.com. Undated. https://tribecafilm.com/stories/attack-the-block-star-john-boyega-star-wars-force-awakens-trailer
3. Myers, Maddy. "John Boyega on Finn's Journey in *The Force Awakens,* Meeting JJ Abrams, & More." *The Mary Sue.* September 2, 2015. http://www.themarysue.com/john-boyega-the-force-awakens/

Chapter 4

1. Lange, Maggie. "Star Wars' John Boyega Preferred the Dark Side as a Kid." *GQ.* December 17, 2015. http://www.gq.com/story/john-boyega-preferred-the-dark-side
2. Milligan, Lauren. "Five Minutes with Film's New Force." *Vogue.* January 7, 2016. http://www.Vogue.co.uk/arts-and-lifestyle/2016/01/john-boyega-interview-star-wars-finn-actor
3. Lange.
4. Ibid.
5. Biglow, Erin. "John Boyega on Telling Family about 'Star Wars' Role: 'My Dad Had No Clue.'" *Access Hollywood.* December 18, 2015. http://www.accesshollywood.com/articles/john-boyega-telling-family-about-star-wars-role-my-dad-had-no-clue/
6. Ibid.
7. Ibid.
8. Lange.
9. Ibid.
10. Milligan.
11. Renwick, Finlay. "John Boyega Interview: 'The Biggest Perk So Far Is Being Let Off a Parking Ticket.'" *Esquire.* January 6, 2016. http://www.esquire.co.uk/culture/film/news/a9301/john-boyega-interview-star-wars/
12. Milligan.
13. Itzkoff, Dave. "In New 'Star Wars,' Daisy Ridley and John Boyega Brace for Galactic Fame." *The New York Times.* December 9, 2015. http://www.nytimes.com/2015/12/20/movies/in-new-star-wars-daisy-ridley-and-john-boyega-brace-for-galactic-fame.html
14. Milligan.

Chapter 5

1. Milligan, Lauren. "Five Minutes with Film's New Force." Vogue. January 7, 2016. http://www.Vogue.co.uk/arts-and-lifestyle/2016/01/john-boyega-interview-star-wars-finn-actor
2. Ibid.
3. Ojomu, Nola. "The Force Is Strong with This One! *Star Wars* Star John Boyega Enjoys Playful Lightsaber Battle with a Young Fan during Charity Visit to a London Hospital." *The Daily Mail.* March 13, 2016. http://www.dailymail.co.uk/tvshowbiz/article-3490502/Stars-Wars-star-John-Boyega-makes-young-fan-s-dream-come-true-charity-visit-London-hospital.html
4. Ibid.
5. Jackson, Marc. "Rising *Star Wars: The Force Awakens* Actor John Boyega Beams as He Beats Brie Larson and Dakota Johnson to Take Home Breakthrough Award at the BAFTAs." *The Daily Mail.* February 14, 2016. http://www.dailymail.co.uk/tvshowbiz/article-3447038/John-Boyega-wins-EE-Rising-Star-award-BAFTAs.html

Books

Fentiman, David. *Star Wars: The Force Awakens: New Adventures.* New York: DK Children, 2015.

Fry, Jason. *Star Wars: The Force Awakens Incredible Cross-Sections.* New York: DK Children. 2015.

Kogge, Michael. *Star Wars: The Force Awakens Junior Novel.* New York: Disney LucasFilm Press, 2016.

Summers, Keira. *"John Boyega: The Star Wars Actor's Rise to Fame."* Tailslating Media, 2015.

Szostak, Phil, and LucasFilm Ltd. *The Art of "Star Wars: The Force Awakens."* New York: Abrams Books, 2015.

On the Internet

John Boyega.net is the "online source for all things John Boyega"
  john-boyega.net

The Force.net is a web site for fans of Star Wars with new stories, interviews and more.
  www.theforce.net

audition (aw-DIH-shun)—To try out for a role.

charismatic (kayr-iz-MAT-ik)—Charming.

debut (day-BYOO)—First public appearance.

fluke (FLOOK)—Accidental success.

franchise (FRAN-chyz)—A store with a license to sell a company's products.

legacy (LEG-uh-see)—Something handed down.

nominate (NAH-mih-nayt)—To suggest someone for an award or position.

prequel (PREE-kwul)—A book or movie that takes place before a previously released book or movie.

rapport (ruh-POOR)—A friendly relationship.

rehearsal (ree-HER-sul)—A practice performance.